CW00731902

Planes and Airports

Fascinating to young and old alike, airports and aeroplanes are familiar but often little understood. Here Chris McAllister gives us the inside story in language we can all handle. Did you know that a Jumbo has a fuel consumption figure of 246 yards per gallon when cruising, or that it guzzles a gallon per second for each engine during take-off? Probably not, but the book tells us this and much more, enough in fact to allow us to appreciate airport activity from landing, servicing, maintenance and take-off to in-flight procedures of navigation, control and performance. Add to this a review of the capabilities of today's airliners and stunning photographs of the planes in action and you have a complete picture of modern flight – one of man's most fascinating and complex achievements.

Chris McAllister is a lecturer in Psychology and Communications Studies at North Cheshire College. He is a dedicated aviation enthusiast; the fact that he grew up under the flight path of Dublin airport's main runway served only to start him off on a life-long hobby!

50 photographs with colour throughout

A BATSFORD PAPERBACK

Planes and Airports

Chris McAllister

B. T. Batsford Ltd, London

To Ann, Jo and Sarah

By the same author
Aircraft Alive –
aviation and air traffic for enthusiasts
Batsford, 1980

© Chris McAllister 1981
First published 1981

All rights reserved. No part of this publication may be
reproduced, in any form or by any means, without permission
from the Publisher.

ISBN 0 7134 3911 4

Typeset by Typewise Ltd, Wembley
and printed in Hong Kong
for the publishers B. T. Batsford Ltd,
4 Fitzhardinge Street, London W1H 0AH

Contents

Frontispiece Passengers boarding via the rear door of a Yugoslav Airlines Boeing 727 *(JAT)*

Acknowledgment
I would like to thank all those many companies and people who supplied me with illustrations or who helped me in any way to put this book together.

The Airport Scene

Airports are about planes and people. The planes are obvious enough, especially the huge Boeing 747 Jumbo which, although it entered service over ten years ago, still has people wondering how anything quite so enormous can lift itself into the air and carry up to 500 passengers or 100 tons of cargo to the far side of the world in a matter of hours.

Then there are the people, most of whom are passengers, especially in summer. They are often accompanied by their friends and relatives, the 'meeters and greeters' who came to the airport to welcome these travellers or to see them off and take the car back home. There are the spectators like you and me, who come to watch the planes, take photographs of them, or listen to the radio chatter on small pocket receivers. Then there are the airport's own people, flight crew and cabin staff, ground workers, customs men, police, clerks, caterers, and a host of others whose job it is to keep the planes flying or to keep all the other people alive, well fed, comfortable and reasonably happy.

Besides planes and people, there is another magic ingredient which is the life-blood of civil aviation, at least in the West. No, you guessed wrong. It isn't fuel, it's money. Planes and airports are expensive to operate. Only a few very rich people or foolish governments can afford to run an airline just for fun, and unless the passenger bookings or cargo fees are enough to pay the bills, no planes would take off, the restaurants and lounges would be empty, and grass would be growing through the cracks in the concrete.

So, there is more to a Concorde, a 747 or an Airbus than a mere piece of technological achievement. In the end it all boils down to money. Each aeroplane is an investment for its owners, a commercial proposition with which they hope to make a profit in these times of soaring fuel prices and mounting inflation. British Airways makes a small profit from its Concorde flights across the North Atlantic, showing that there are just about enough people prepared

to pay the extra costs not only for the shortened journey time and the privilege of flying supersonic, but also for the exclusive VIP treatment they receive. At the other end of the scale, it is possible to pack so many people into a 747 that they can fly to New York for a fare that works out at less than 2½ pence per passenger mile at the time of writing. Most motorists, if they were honest with themselves, would have to agree that their family cars cost far more than that to run. And with air travel, there is the convenience of being able to travel quickly and directly from A to B, spanning oceans and mountain ranges and avoiding much of the tedium of surface travel.

Sitting there on the apron in front of the terminal, the Jumbo is so big that people invariably find themselves asking questions about it. The physical dimensions are obvious enough: length 231 feet, wingspan 196 feet. Other planes in the past have been as big, if not bigger, but it is weight and lifting ability that really matter. When empty, most 747s weigh around 170 metric tonnes. The cargo versions can load up with 113 tonnes maximum. The highest density passenger layout has room for 500 seats, with a lower deck for baggage and cargo besides. There are ten doors, twelve toilets and six galleys. The fuel tanks can hold nearly 200,000 litres (43,000 gallons) of aviation kerosene, weighing 156 tonnes. The plane can be loaded to capacity either with maximum cargo, or maximum fuel, but not both, because all-up take-off weight has to be restricted to 363 tonnes.

In this fuel-conscious age you find yourself wondering how far your car would travel on 43,000 gallons, especially if it ran on kerosene, which packs more power than petrol. But the 747 manages about 6000 miles to the tankful. This works out at 246 yards per gallon, a distance which the plane covers in less than a second while it cruises at nearly 600 mph at a height of 35,000 feet. However, during take-off, when maximum power is needed, *each one* of the four huge turbofan engines guzzles almost a gallon a second while it strains at the leash to the tune of 23 tonnes per engine.

The Boeing 747. It still amazes people that anything quite so big and heavy can take off and fly *(A British Airways Photograph)*

Another popular Boeing, the twin-jet 737 *(Aer Lingus)*

In contrast, a smaller but still very familiar Boeing, the twin-jet 737, has less than half the span or length of its huge cousin, weighs only 27 tonnes empty and 52 tonnes all-up. Payload is 130 passengers or the equivalent amount of cargo. The two engines develop 6½ tonnes thrust apiece, enabling the plane to climb as high and fly almost as fast as the Jumbo. The range of the 737 is only 2500 miles and the fuel tankage is considerably smaller; a mere 4300 gallons (15.6 tonnes), one-tenth the capacity of the huge 'Seven Forty Seven'.

These vital statistics for the 747 Jumbo are mind-boggling until you put them in perspective. The huge plane's awesome thirst begins to make sense when you divide it by the payload it is designed to carry, whether hundreds of passengers or tons of cargo, then the sums begin to come out right. The 747 is an economical aeroplane compared with its predecessors, and some newer planes such as the Airbus A300 and A310 are even more economical. What *doesn't* make economic sense is to have these huge planes flying around half-empty or to have them sitting on the ground when they should be in the air earning money.

There are different ways of running an airline. For decades the scheduled passenger service has been the backbone of commercial aviation - regular and dependable if not always profitable. It is becoming fashionable to 'knock' the scheduled airlines on account of various shortcomings, real or imagined: inefficiency, over-manning, high fares, empty seats. True, many of the scheduled airlines are, except in the US, heavily state-subsidized symbols of national prestige; but for the record, our own British Airways is more efficient than most, and manages to pay its way even in these hard times. Unlike the holiday airlines, which can fill their planes by creaming off the most popular destinations during the most popular seasons, the scheduled operators have to maintain a service throughout the year. Moscow in winter isn't a very heart-warming place, but some people still need to go there, and it isn't very heart-warming or consoling either to watch a 100- seater jet arrive at a British airport on a bleak winter's night to disembark all of six passengers, including two infants and a dog. At a time of high fuel costs, it is embarrassing for any airline to have empty seats on its hands.

An alternative to the scheduled-airline way of doing business is the charter system. Planes take off fully booked

A BAC One-Eleven in the livery of Air UK is marshalled to a stop at Norwich *(Air UK)*

Laker's DC-10 'Skytrain' offers fully bookable, no-fuss, low-cost airfares on some routes *(Laker Airways)*

Right A view of Gatwick Airport showing the terminal buildings and spectator terraces, loading piers and jetties, aircraft parked on the apron and in the distance the main runway *(British Caledonian Airways)*

on every flight; therefore low fares can be offered, generating a whole new mass-market in air travel. The holiday airlines have long since abandoned their secondhand image. Companies such as Laker, Britannia, Dan-Air, Orion and Air Europe use brand-new planes, which passengers prefer, but which also require less maintenance and are easier to keep flying during the busy summer season.

Companies in the low-fare business, such as Laker, are frequently held up as an object-lesson to the scheduled operators such as British Airways, and to the general public Sir Freddie Laker is a hero, a knight in a shining DC-10. But the comparison is not quite so simple. It is the scheduled airlines which have over the years developed the planes, the routes, the airports and the service, and in hard times we depend on them to keep the planes, and the flag, flying. The holiday airlines have found a whole new market for low-cost air travel, a market which also benefits the scheduled carriers in different ways. They too can run their

own holiday operations, British Airtours being one example, or they can sell otherwise empty seats by offering Standby, ABC, APEX or other reduced fares. The complex fare systems can create anomalies, as when the cheapest way of flying from London to Copenhagen is via New York!

It is not just the airlines, but the airports themselves which have to pay their way. Most British airports are operated by the British Airports Authority or by some other public body which has to meet its costs by charging the airport's users. Aircraft pay landing fees, ramp fees and overnight fees. People visiting the airport pay when they park their cars, buy refreshments or other goods in the airport's shops, or even when they are charged a small fee to get onto the terraces to watch the planes.

Aeroplane watching is a surprisingly popular pastime, and most airports provide facilities for spectators, those who come to meet and greet passengers, watch visiting pop stars etc., as well as those whose interest is more strictly aeronautical. The piers and terraces are usually open from about nine or ten in the morning until dusk. At other times alternative vantage points are not too hard to find, such as the airport perimeter or the top deck of the multi-storey car park. Beware, however. During a security crisis, if you are not a passenger you may find it difficult to get near the airport at all.

If you are looking for airport activity, remember that scheduled flights are most frequent in the morning, at about breakfast-time, and again in the early evening. At some airports, early afternoon in particular is a disappointingly slack time. Again, at some airports you can get nearer the planes than at others. At Manchester International, spectators can walk out along the roofs of the piers close to the aircraft, take photographs easily and watch all stages of arrival, turnround and departure.

And now, the scene behind the scenes. In order to protect governments and airlines as well as the travelling public, civil air transport is governed by a whole host of internationally agreed regulations which have the force of law in each country. In Britain, civil air transport is regulated on behalf of the government by the Civil Aviation Authority, a powerful body which referees competition between airlines, enforces the law of the air, maintains the navigation and air-traffic control systems, checks that airlines can operate safely, that planes are airworthy and that pilots are licensed and medically fit to fly. With the CAA about, no-one could lease an old biplane, offer cheap trips to the Isle of Wight and call himself an airline pilot, which is probably just as well!

Planes and Engines

The first aeroplane, the Wright Brothers' *Flyer I*, took to the air on 17 December 1903. Now it would look distinctly odd, if as you were watching, a replica of this flimsy biplane landed on the main runway and taxied up to park itself alongside the big jets on the apron. Yet this rickety wire and canvas kite is the direct ancestor of today's sleek metal monsters, despite their powerful engines and their insides brimming with multiple electrical and hydraulic systems and complicated radio and electronics. Spanning the eight decades in between was a process of gradual development during which we learned, often the hard way, how to transform aeroplanes into airliners, that is, how to take the Wright Brothers' invention and turn it into something which would make a profit for its owners by carrying passengers. An important milestone in this process of development was an aeroplane which took to the air on 17 December 1935, exactly 32 years after *Flyer I*, a plane which surely got to be just as famous, the Douglas DC-3.

The few remaining DC-3 Dakotas are probably the oldest transport planes you are likely to see parked at the airports or droning around the air lanes these days. There are still a few on the UK register and they do mail and cargo work. The DC-3 became a legend in its lifetime whether in or out of warpaint or serving with just about every airline in the world in the lean years after World War II. Powered by two 1200 hp nine-cylinder air-cooled engines, the Dakota represented- in its day all the virtues of the successful airliner. It was fast, safe, roomy, reliable, economical and popular with crews and passengers alike.

They never did find a replacement for the Dakota, or rather they never did agree as to which plane had taken its place. Was it Britain's successful Vickers Viscount, the first turbine-powered airliner, which went into service in 1953? But the Viscount was in a different league; compared to the Dakota it had twice the power, could carry twice as many passengers in pressurized comfort twice as high and at twice the speed, and most important of all it had gas-turbine engines. The Viscount sold well and introduced the world's airports to the smell of kerosene.

The petrol-burning piston-driven aero engine had reached the peak of its development. More power meant even more cylinders (some engines had as many as 28). There were difficulties from vibration and with cooling and lubricating these complicated and overstretched engines full of metal parts which clattered to and fro, prone to wear and needing frequent overhauls. The jet engine, the first of the gas turbines, had appeared during the war, and was being developed for fighter planes which now set new speed and altitude records and began punching holes in the sound barrier itself.

The principle of the gas turbine had been understood for some time, but new alloys needed to be developed which would withstand the high temperatures involved. At the cool, front end of the engine a multi-blade rotating compressor sucks in large volumes of air which it compresses up to four times. This compressed air is then mixed with kerosene and burned to produce a large volume of very hot gas at the same high pressure. This is what pushes the jet engine (and the plane) forward, and as the hot gases escape from the rear of the engine, they spin the turbine blades which power the compressor at the front.

Of course, getting rid of the propeller made higher speeds and altitudes possible, but for civil aviation the immediate advantage of the new turbine engines was their simplicity. Almost the only important moving part was the *spool*, that is the turbine/compressor assembly and the connecting shaft. Turbines rarely break down, use very little oil, cool themselves, and need much less maintenance than piston engines. But the airlines were not yet ready to propel passengers around the sky at 500 mph. The jet engine had to be tamed first and this was done by bringing back the propeller and gearing it to the front end of the spool. A larger turbine was used so as to absorb most of the power of the jet exhaust, and the result was the propjet or turboprop engine, such as the Rolls Royce Dart which powers the Viscount.

The early Dart turboprops produced 1540 hp, but by a process of development which has become familiar, this was 'stretched' or 'uprated' in later versions of the engine to over 2000 hp without any significant increase in size or weight. Thus the later, more powerful Darts were used in the later and bigger 800 and 810 series Viscounts which had bigger cabins to carry more passengers.

The uprated Darts were also chosen to power the smaller twin-engined turboprop airliners which appeared in the late 1950s and early 60s, such as the low-wing British Aerospace HS 748, and the pretty, high-wing Fokker F-27 Friendship. Both types are still in production and selling well, and have inspired imitations. Compare the HS 748 with its Japanese counterpart, the NAMC YS-11, and compare the Friendship with the very similar Handley Page Herald or the Soviet Antonov An-24.

The Douglas DC-3 Dakota, of 1935 vintage, was the first successful airliner to be produced in large numbers. This one still flies from Humberside Airport on cargo work *(Eastern Airways)*

Right Two popular Rolls Royce Dart engined turboprop airliners:
Above Fokker F-27 Friendship *(Air UK)*
Below Vickers Viscount 800 series *(British Midland Airways)*

The pure jet engine went into airline service in the ill-fated De Havilland Comet I, which was withdrawn from service in 1954 following disastrous crashes found to be due to metal fatigue. So the only jet airliner in use between 1954 and 1958 was the Russian Tu-104, very much a converted bomber!

In 1958 another of the truly great aeroplanes of all time was ready to join the airlines, the American-built Boeing 707. This was bigger and faster than the later Comets, and had the range to cross the Atlantic. Nearly 1000 were built,

in a variety of different models. Another big four-jet which appeared about the same time was the DC-8, which at first looked like the Boeing 707, but as more powerful engines became available, the DC-8 was stretched and stretched until the later McDonnell Douglas DC-8 Super 60 series came to look like flying pencils, with accommodation for up to 259 passengers in their long cabins.

The success of the French Caravelle set a fashion for rear-mounted engines and T-tails, and in the 1960s a large number of new designs appeared, some with two engines at the rear (BAC One-Eleven, Fokker F-28 Fellowship, McDonnell Douglas DC-9, Tupolev 134), some with three engines at the rear (Trident, Boeing 727, Tupolev 154), and

The Handley Page Herald, powered by two Rolls Royce Dart turboprops *(Air UK)*

Boeing 707-320C *(British Caledonian Airways)*

two with four rear-mounted engines: the VC-10, Britain's hopeful answer to the Boeing 707, and its Soviet look-alike, the Ilyushin 62, still the basis of Aeroflot's long-haul routes. All these new designs were powered by the latest development of the gas-turbine engine, the *turbofan.*

Just as the turboprop is a gas-turbine engine with a propeller geared to the front of the spool, the turbofan has, in place of the prop, a large multi-blade fan spinning inside a duct or casing. Only a proportion of the air collected by the fan is passed to the compressor for further treatment in the engine's hot core. Most of the air from the fan misses the core altogether, so the early turbofans were called *by-pass* engines. Nowadays the fan-gearbox is driven from a second, more powerful turbine and spool, shafted inside the first, hence the term *two-spool* engine.

The huge 'advanced technology turbofans' such as the Pratt and Whitney JT9D, the General Electric CF6 and the Rolls Royce RB-211, all of which are roughly the same size

The trend-setting Aerospatiale Caravelle was the first of the rear-engined jets

Right Twin-engined T-tail jets compared:
Above BAC One-Eleven Series 200 *(British Caledonian Airways)*
Below McDonnell-Douglas DC-9-14 *(British Midland Airways)*

and are used to power today's wide-bodied jets, have fans so big that only about one-fifth of the air they swallow goes through the core.

It is of course the fan which is doing most of the work of pulling the plane forward and transmitting much of the engine's power, just like the propeller of a turboprop. However, propellers are happiest at speeds below 400 mph and below 25,000 feet, and pure jets prefer flying at over 1000 mph high in the stratosphere. For this reason, Concorde's Olympus engines are pure jets. But for speeds around 500-600 mph and altitudes around 35,000 feet which suit most of today's airliners, the turbofan is the best compromise between the propeller and the jet. It's easy on fuel, cleaner because the burners can be regulated better, and quieter because the roar of the jet exhaust is being tamed by the fan. The success of today's big jets is due almost entirely to the development of the turbofan.

So, powered by four huge Pratt and Whitney JT9D turbofans, the Boeing 747 astounded the world when it went into service in 1969 and was affectionately christened 'Jumbo.' A year or two later this monster was joined by two more, the McDonnell Douglas DC-10 powered by three General Electric CF6 turbofans and the Lockheed L-1011 Tristar powered by three Rolls Royce RB-211s. The development of the superb three-spool RB-211 turbofan nearly brought about the collapse of Rolls Royce and got the Tristar off to a shaky start, but those airlines which operate Tristars are very pleased with them, including British Airways which has now bought a number of the later, longer-range Tristar 500s. The RB-211s have proved to be economical, quiet engines, and are also available on some versions of the Boeing 747.

The new big planes were popular with passengers, who liked the wider looking cabins with their more spacious seating and higher ceilings. There was no longer the impression of being crowded into a narrow tube, and wide-screen movies could be shown on the longer flights.

In 1972 the Airbus A300 made its first flight, built by a new consortium, Airbus Industrie, in different places all over Europe and put together at Toulouse around a pair of CF6 engines. The cynics were dubious. Another plane designed by a committee, they said; it won't fly. And then when it did fly they said it wouldn't sell. But the Airbus proved them wrong.

Clearly there was going to be a slot in the market for a short/medium range airliner built to fly on two of the new large engines, but at first nobody saw this. How could anyone dare to challenge the supremacy of mighty Boeing, least of all an international consortium, following all the ballyhoo that the Anglo-French Concorde had engendered? But if Concorde represents the supreme technical achievement of European co-operation, Airbus represents its supreme commercial achievement.

Because it does not have to carry the large amounts of fuel

Left Tupolev Tu-134A *(Czechoslovak Airlines)*

A Boeing 727 in the colourful livery of Spain's national airline *(Iberia)*

Above The BAC Super VC-10 has four rear-mounted engines *(A British Airways Photograph)*, as does its Soviet-built look-alike, the Ilyushin Il-62M, *below (Janusz Czerniak, LOT Polish Airlines)*

Right Boeing 747SP. This 'Special Performance' shortened version of the 747 is designed for long-range low-density routes *(PAN AM)*

of its main rivals, and also because of its very advanced wing, the Airbus can do on two engines what the others do on three. Soon after its introduction into service by Air France, that company was claiming a 30 per cent reduction in operating costs, compared with its older planes. This sent the customers flocking to Toulouse, and Airbus Industrie is sure of a big future as a plane maker. The smaller A310 Airbus will soon follow the A300 into service, and even more Airbuses are planned in varying sizes – the even bigger TA9 and the long-range TA11. For less dense routes Airbus will be offering the single-aisle SA range, seating 120-170 passengers. If imitation is the sincerest form of flattery, the new Boeings, the 767 and 757 are aimed at exactly the same slots in the market and look remarkably similar to the Airbus family.

What makes the Airbus so economical is, in the first place, the advanced CF6 turbofan engines, but in the second place the wing, which is designed and built by British Aerospace, the most efficient and advanced wing of any airliner in service. At present four wings per month are built at Chester and flown out of Manchester each weekend in a special Super Guppy freighter. In similar fashion the

Second largest of the wide-bodied jets, the McDonnell-Douglas DC-10 *(British Caledonian Airways)*

Right Lockheed L-1011 Tristar 500. Note how the positioning of the third engine in the tail compares with that on the DC-10 *(A British Airways Photograph)*

fuselage is flown to Toulouse from Hamburg and Bremen, and other parts arrive from Madrid, Amsterdam and Saint-Nazaire.

The Russians too, have a wide-bodied airliner, the 350-seater Ilyushin Il-86, comparable in size to the A300 Airbus, but as the USSR has no big turbofan in the 20-25 tonne category, this plane is powered by four 13-tonne Kuznetsov turbofans. At the time of writing the Il-86 has begun service on Soviet internal routes, and may soon be a regular visitor to West European airports.

And what of the future? Disappointing though it may seem, the next decade or two is unlikely to produce too many revolutionary new shapes in the sky. The new planes will resemble very closely those we have at present, and will look even more like one another. The new engines will be developed versions of those of today. The changes, though hidden, will be important; for instance, fuel economy. Anything which promises to gain a few more yards per gallon will be incorporated in the new designs.

For example, lightening the structure is one obvious way

Close-up of a Rolls Royce RB-211 turbofan fitted to a Lockheed Tristar *(A British Airways Photograph)*

Right A300 Airbus. European collaboration has produced a winner *(Air France)*

The extra space and headroom provided by the big, new, wide-bodied jets is an important selling point with passengers
(British Caledonian Airways)

to improve fuel economy. New alloys, new structures such as honeycombed metal panels, new materials such as plastic reinforced with glass fibre, carbon fibre, Kevlar, etc., are being used increasingly on planes, and this trend is likely to continue.

Other improvements will involve the increasing use of microelectronics, computing and digital techniques embracing all aspects of airliner operation. New super-intelligent autopilots will keep planes stable and on course without the need for large fuel-wasting tail surfaces. Computerized flight decks with video displays will take over from today's clutter of separate instruments, simplifying the flying, the navigation and the fuel

The Airbus A300B4. The complicated high-lift devices, the flaps and slats fitted to this aircraft's wing, combined with the advanced design of the wing itself are part of the secret of the plane's success *(Alitalia)*

management. Improved air-traffic control systems will cut out the time and fuel wasted while approaching to land at busy airports, and automatic landing in zero visibility (Category 3 conditions) will become more and more commonplace.

Finally, if and when the oil does run out, it is probable that alternative fuels (methane, methanol, liquid hydrogen) will have been developed.

'Announcing the Arrival of…'

It pays to fly as high as possible for as far as possible. The air is thinner up there, so it takes less fuel to push the plane along. But when it comes to getting down again, the descent must be judged properly if all this fuel-saving is not to be wasted. The idea should be to coast down a nicely judged slope, letting gravity do some of the work, a slope of about 3°, which will work out at 300 feet of descent per mile. So if you are cruising at 30,000 feet you will want to start your descent 100 miles out, if Air Traffic Control will let you.

'Roger. Cleared to one four zero to maintain.'

You descend to 14,000 feet, only to find that you have to fly level while you await further instructions from the controller.

'Midland Five Eight One. You are cleared to Bovingdon at flight level eight zero to take up the hold.'

So now you know. As expected, Heathrow approach is busy, they're queueing up to land and you have to take your place in the queue. You cross the Bovingdon radio beacon at 8000 feet and immediately start flying the precise racetrack-shaped holding pattern above Hemel Hempstead. You're in the stack, and there will be other planes stacked above and below you with 1000 feet of sky between each.

You're not the pilot, but you can get the feel of what it's like up there easily enough. Many aviation enthusiasts buy themselves a small pocket-sized radio which can be tuned to the civil air band (108-136 MHz) and eavesdrop on pilots and controllers talking to each other. You need to learn what the local aircraft frequencies are, plus a smattering of the radio jargon, and you find yourself listening in to the fascinating world of the flight deck, gaining an insight into the mysteries of instrument flying and radio navigation*. But first, just one word of caution about the use of air-band radios. Listening-in is technically illegal in the UK, but if you looked around you at an airport you would never guess this!

*Aircraft Alive: aviation and air traffic for enthusiasts, by Chris McAllister, Batsford, 1980.

Laypeople who are allowed the privilege of flying on the flight deck of an airliner and peering over the pilot's shoulder are often surprised to find that when they break out of the bottom of the cloud during an approach, the runway and its lights are already perfectly lined up straight in front of them. Which is as it should be. The mass of radio beacons and other approach aids which surround a modern airport make it a straightforward business for a pilot to find the runway and line up with it in all kinds of weather, even if he has never landed there before. A pilot can use the radio aids to approach to within a few hundred feet of the runway. From there he should be able to see what he's doing, but if he is still in cloud or fog, he is supposed to overshoot, go round again, or divert to another airfield where the weather is better. Modern aircraft are capable of fully automatic blind landings in fog, provided certain other conditions are certified as OK.

The main radio aid used in landing is the Instrument Landing System or ILS. This provides a pattern of radio beams which mark the approach to the runway down a 3° slope. The most prominent part of the ILS is the *localizer transmitter,* a yellow fence-like structure at the far end of the runway. This provides an accurately calibrated radio beam which extends along the centreline of the runway and out into the country for miles beyond. The 3° glideslope is marked by another pattern of beams radiated from a small tower close to the touchdown end of the runway. As the plane approaches the carefully aligned beams, pointers on dials on the flight deck will begin to swing towards the centre. If the pilot now flies the plane so as to keep the pointers central, he should fly down the centre of the beam for miles, straight onto the runway. He is, as he would say, 'established on the ILS.' He can also let the autopilot fly the ILS for him, locked onto the radio signals.

Usually on the ILS approach, there are two *marker* beacons which produce a bleeping noise in the pilot's headset as he flies over them. The Outer Marker is usually positioned about four miles out from the runway, and the

Airborne appendages:
Above left What a lot of wheels! A Boeing 747 'dangles the Dunlops' *(A British Airways Photograph)*
Below left Leading-edge slats on a Tristar *(A British Airways Photograph)*

Above right Wheel-bay fairings, Tupolev Tu-154
Below right Triple-slotted flaps, Boeing 747

The Big Four approaching to land:
Above left Boeing 747 *(A British Airways Photograph)*
Below left Lockheed Tristar *(A British Airways Photograph)*

Above right McDonnell-Douglas DC-10 *(Lufthansa)*
Below right Airbus A300

Middle Marker is less than one mile out. They warn the pilot that he is getting close, and that the plane should now be in landing trim, wheels and flaps down.

A pilot could easily find the ILS and land on it without any assistance from a controller, but this assumes that nobody else is trying to do the same thing at the same precise moment. The approach controller's job is to keep planes clear of each other and to feed them onto the ILS one by one. Normally he uses radar to help him.

'Midland Five Eight One is cleared to land. Runway Two Eight Right. Wind three one zero, five knots.'

'Speedbird Seven Four, report Outer Marker.'

'Transworld Seven Zero Six. You're number three in traffic. Can you slow down, please?'

'Thai Nine One Four, steer two four zero to close with the localizer for a ten-mile final and report established.'

Planes landing at the rate of one a minute keep the Heathrow controllers busy, as you can see for yourself if you look for a vantage point beyond the end of the runway, just under the approach. The planes passing close above your head will be easy to photograph if you fancy them dangling all those wheels and flaps. Now look out along the approach. There seems to be an invisible set of rails in the sky, stretching out for miles dead straight and up at an angle of 3° with planes sliding down these rails one after the other. One of the planes might happen to be a red, white and black HS 748 belonging to the Civil Aviation Authority, busy doing its regular job of flying the beams just to check that they are still straight and correctly aligned.

Meanwhile back in the cockpit, the two pilots are busy complying with all the radioed instructions. They must judge the best moment to start slowing the plane down and to lower the wheels and flaps. These appendages slow the plane anyway, and the job of the flaps and slats is to coax extra lift from the wings to compensate for the loss in speed. A plane could land without using flaps – at something like 200 mph – but it would need a long runway on which to slow down afterwards.

A modern airliner is a complicated machine full of powerful hydraulic systems, electric motors and screwjacks etc., which move the control surfaces on the wings and tail, raise and lower the wheels and undercarriage doors, push the huge trailing–edge flaps and leading–edge slats out on their hinges or sliding in their curved tracks, cushion the touchdown, spring open the airbrakes on the top of the wing, open the doors and sliding panels for the engines to reverse their thrust, and finally bring the whole 250 tonnes to rest by stamping on the wheelbrakes. Improvements in the machinery are just as important as improvements in engines or in aerodynamics. The Boeing 747 has complex triple-slotted flaps to lower the landing and take-off speeds, whereas the wing of the Airbus, from root to tip, in front and behind, is cluttered with high-lift gadgetry, an important ingredient in the plane's success, enabling it to take off and land using fairly short runways on only two engines, whereas its rivals need three or four. The flaps and slats are not only impressive on all the big, wide-bodied planes, they are also a useful recognition feature.

So the pilot aims to fly the descent and most of the approach 'clean' and only 'dangles the Dunlops' and sticks out the flaps when he has to in order to slow down. Dragging all that clobber through the sky uses a lot of fuel. However, by the time the plane has reached the Outer Marker on final approach, about four miles out, the plane should be in landing trim, and all pre-landing checks should be completed. The thing now is to use the power levers to control the speed so that the plane arrives over the end of the runway, travelling only a few knots above its landing speed. In gusty conditions (wind shear) a faster approach is advisable, and you may see the plane rolling in the turbulence or yawing to control a strong crosswind.

Once he is safely over the runway threshold the pilot knows he has made it, and can now pull the engines right back to idling speed. He pulls back on the wheel to bring the nose up slightly and 'round out' the landing. The plane coasts for several hundred yards, skimming over the runway before finally touching down at a speed which for most modern types will be around 120 mph. There is a short scream from the tyres and a plume of smoke as a layer of rubber is burnt off wheels which were stationary just a second ago, and have now been spun up to full rolling speed.

And now this hunk of speeding metal has to be slowed down and brought to a halt before it runs out of concrete. First the air-brakes, sometimes called *spoilers*, pop up from the top of the wing, the nosewheel touches down, and the

A layer of rubber is singed from a Concorde's tyres as the sleek bird touches down at 140 mph. Each tyre survives about 40 such landings *(A British Airways Photograph)*

weight of the plane is gradually transferred from the wings to the wheels. The nosewheel can now be used to steer the plane and the wheelbrakes can be used to stop it.

But not just yet. Aeroplanes brakes, though powerful, are quite small. Slammed on hard at these speeds, they would get hot enough to start a fire, so the pilot uses thrust-reversers first.

On the smaller jets thrust is reversed by using a pair of clamshell doors to block off the tailpipe and the exhaust escapes through vanes which open in the side of the engine. Full power is used again and the plane is effectively slowed down in a cloud of black smoke.

On the big turbofan engines an ingenious system is used

Slowing a DC-10. Notice the spoilers (airbrakes) which have hinged upwards from the top of the wings, and the dark ring around each engine where the casing has moved back to expose the thrust reversing cascades *(KLM)*

to reverse the blast from the fans. A ring of doors closes to block off the rear end of the fan duct. Now watch the fan casings. Notice how the rear section of each casing slides back to expose a set of small vents called cascades, designed to deflect the fan blast forwards. For a few seconds the engines roar up to full power again, then the fan casings slide shut once more. Now the plane is moving slowly enough for the brakes to be used without much risk of overheating. Cooler brakes would mean using bigger wheels, adding weight and bulk. As it is, tyres need to be changed after about 60 braked landings and 40 in the case of Concorde because of the higher speeds involved.

Once the plane has slowed down, it turns off the main runway under instructions from the tower or from the ground controller. It then has to navigate a maze of taxiways to its allocated parking position on the apron in front of the terminal. Look for indicator boards, traffic lights, or even an illuminated vehicle sporting a big flashing sign 'Follow Me'! A Marshaller with coloured bats will guide the big plane over the last few yards and help it to park neatly. Then your ears can hear again as the turbines are switched off, run down and finally stop.

Turnround

The idea behind the 'bus stop jets' is that they should be fast on the ground as well as in the air. If they can only earn their keep when they are flying, then they should be able to turnround as quickly as possible and take off again with another load of passengers or cargo. Most of the short- or medium-range jets are designed with this in mind and they incorporate a number of features to speed up the turnround. For example, many of these planes have their own set of passenger steps, or airstairs, which rattle to the ground as soon as the engines are stopped.

Normally, once the engines have stopped, the aircraft's systems would have to work off the batteries, until a noisy, diesel-driven generator called a Ground Power Unit (GPU) can be brought along and plugged in. To avoid having to wait for a GPU to arrive, most jets nowadays have a small turbine, called an Auxiliary Power Unit (APU) which is kept running during the turnround to keep the pumps, generators, air conditioning, etc. working without draining the batteries. The APU is usually mounted in the tail and exhausts through a small jetpipe near the base of the rudder. Although they are supposed to be small turbines, some APUs, such as those on the BAC One-Eleven make an awful lot of noise.

Clearly, there is a lot of work to be done during the turnround. Passengers, luggage and cargo have to be unloaded. Refuelling and revictualling has to be arranged. The plane has to be tidied, perhaps cleaned, and minor repairs may need to be attended to, such as changing a soiled seatcover or replacing a small lightbulb. The embarking passengers and their baggage have to be checked in and the outgoing cargo has to be loaded carefully. And then there are the inevitable odd bits of paperwork to sort out.

This is called Ground Handling and somebody has to take charge of it. If an airline doesn't have its own handling facilities on the spot, it will pay a local company to do it for them. For example Servisair Limited does most of the handling for the independent airlines.

British Airways do their own handling wherever possible, employing red-hatted flight dispatchers who have full charge of the whole operation. As the plane's doors open and as the steps or jetty is fixed in position, the 'redcap' is there to welcome it, receive the necessary documents, cargo manifest and so on. He will know already how much fuel is needed and what else needs to be done before the flight leaves again. He will know how many passengers are due to board the plane for the return flight, and whether there are any special problems. He is in charge of loading the cargo, and of preparing a Load and Trim sheet which will tell the captain how heavy his plane is and how evenly this weight is distributed.

The airlines regard punctuality as very important, ranking second only to safety. If delays do occur, quick turnrounds may be the only way of catching up lost time. The scheduled airlines usually plan their operations so as to leave quite a bit of slack, so you won't see lightning turnrounds very often. But the holiday airlines, shuttling back and forth between here and sunny Spain, know that any delay is likely to have a 'knock-on' effect unless they happen to have a spare aircraft available, and they try to make up time on turnrounds whenever they can.

It is possible to turn a plane around in five minutes. Dan Air operate an Inter City 'bus run' around the regional airports using HS 748s, and they have been known to arrive and depart within five minutes, leaving the starboard engine running while on the ground. With a typical short-haul turnround, 20 minutes might be about par for the course. With a long-haul jet, the schedules leave generous turnround time anyway.

In order to be popular with passengers, flights must arrive and depart at convenient times. Thus airports tend to be busier at certain times of the day. Businessmen will prefer to be on the move in the morning and again in the late afternoon. Transatlantic flights are timed to leave the eastern seaboard of North America at about 6 or 7 p.m. (their time) in order to arrive in Europe at around 6 or 7

One of the first of the 'bus-stop' jets, the BAC One-Eleven has its own built-in airstairs and Auxiliary Power Unit (APU) turbine

a.m. the following morning – a seven-hour flight plus a five-hour time difference. They will disembark their bleary-eyed passengers whose bodies will think it is still the middle of the night! The planes must be ready to return from about 11 a.m. onwards, so as to arrive back in the US at about 2 p.m. their time, ready for yet another trip by 6 p.m. that evening!

A plane on the ground which is loading or unloading gets to be surrounded by all manner of vehicles. Airstairs, Customs, cleaners, caterers, bonded stores, cargo-loaders, baggage trucks, power units, fuel tankers and ramp cars, etc. etc. The passenger doors are on the port side of the plane, and the doors on the starboard side give access to the cargo and baggage holds, the galleys, stores and toilets. These last three are level with the cabin, and are reached by means of a truck called a High-Load which lifts up by using an x-shaped jack.

The galley is fully replenished between flights. Refreshments are supplied in aluminium boxes which fit into cabin trolleys. The old boxes are unloaded and new

The cabin staff of a PAN AM Tristar display their latest uniforms
(PAN AM)

ones taken on board. The bonded stores may have to be changed over, because the rule is for duty-free liquor and tobacco to go aboard flights overseas, and for duty-paid items only, to be available on domestic flights. The two must be kept separate.

Although most airlines operate special freighter services, with freight specially palleted and containerized into shapes which fit the aircraft's cabin, there is usually room for general cargo to be taken aboard most passenger flights, if weight and trim permit. The baggage holds are used for this purpose. They are under the floor of the passenger cabin, and are heated and pressurized to the same standards – not for the benefit of stowaways, but for the sake of the small livestock often carried.

Airports use special techniques for handling the millions of gallons of fuel they pump into aircraft tanks. At the bigger airports the fuel comes direct by pipeline from the refinery to the tank farm, and from there it is pressure-fed through a network of pipes to the hydrants dotted around the apron where the planes park. The hydrant covers are flush with the surface of the concrete, so you may not have noticed them as yet. A vehicle called a Ramp Car, full of pipes, valves, filters and dials, plugs one hose into the hydrant and another into the aircraft's refuelling points. The fuel tanks, located in the wings and the belly of the plane under the wings, can all be filled on the more modern planes from a single refuelling point. The hoses are connected by means of self-sealing couplings, which prevent spillage and keep out air, water and dirt, so there is always fuel under pressure, never air, in the pipelines under the concrete, in the hose leading from the hydrant, in the maze of pipes and filters on the ramp car, and in the heavy hoses leading to the plane itself.

Pressure refuelling is capable of delivering 1000 gallons, that is four tons of fuel, per minute from each hydrant, but even so, it would still take nearly an hour to fill up a Jumbo's tanks. The fuel tankers you see trotting round the apron hold only 10,000 gallons apiece; enough to refuel a smaller jet two and a half times, but it would need four tankers to satisfy a 747!

At every stage of the process until finally it is pumped

A popular holiday jet, the Boeing 737 *(Air Europe)*

into the aircraft's tanks, the fuel is filtered and checked for contamination. The most likely impurity will be water, but this is heavier than fuel, and will settle at the bottom of the tanks where it can be drained off through special sumps. Even the aircraft's tanks have these water drains. A small amount of water in the fuel is unlikely to cause engine failure. What can happen is that a species of fungus can get inside the tanks and live and multiply happily on the boundary between the water and the fuel!

Running an airline has hardly ever been an easy way of becoming wealthy, and the problems at the present day are made worse by the sharp increase in the cost of fuel – a more than six-fold increase in less than ten years. Even so it still costs the airlines less per gallon than the petrol we buy from the garage – so in the good old days before the 'oil crisis' they must have been getting it really cheaply, just as we were. And again, the future seems far from assured. How much more is the price of fuel going to rise? Will civil aviation be able to stay in business at all?

Paradoxically, more expensive fuel has led to cheaper air

Powered by two Rolls Royce Dart turboprops, the British Aerospace 748 is a rugged and economical small airliner which seats up to 48 passengers. The largest fleet of 748s in Britain is operated by Dan Air Services Ltd

Maintenance goes on around the clock, seven days a week.
A DC-10 outside its new hangar at Gatwick *(British Caledonian Airways)*

fares! Airlines are finding it more and more vital to fill their planes, and fare-cutting on some routes is a way of doing this. The airports are full of big aeroplanes, and the terminals are swarming with passengers taking advantage of the wonderful value for money that air travel represents today. Maybe that exclusive VIP treatment has gone, those little touches of personal service which were a hangover from the days when air travel was for the wealthy few. Today the wealthy few own their own planes, and the mass market in air travel is buoyant, but there is a nagging fear that it is being kept aloft by a dangerous bubble which may burst only too soon.

Maintenance during the turnround is straightforward. A few simple checks are all that is normally required. Although turbine engines are reliable, they drive pumps and generators which are sometimes checked between flights. On the RB-211 for example, all this 'plumbing' is conveniently located in the fan casing, behind hinged panels where it can be readily inspected. If planes return to

Right Soviet medium-range airliners. *Above* The Tupolev Tu-134A *(Aviogenex) and below* the big, handsome Tupolev Tu-154B which can easily stand comparison with its Western counterparts, the Trident or the Boeing 727

The Fokker F-28 Fellowship is the newest and smallest of the T-tail airliners to be produced in the West. Built in Holland and powered by Rolls Royce Spey turbofans, it is most regularly seen at British airports in the colours of the Dutch operator NLM, and is particularly suited to shorter routes. Note the reduced sweepback and the large flap-track fairings as compared with other types *(NLM Cityhopper)*

their home base for the night, they can receive more immediate attention in the hangars before being rolled out again in time for the following morning. There are bigger overhauls at intervals, and every few years when it has completed tens of thousands of flying hours, the whole plane is stripped down and minutely examined. Eddy currents, ultrasonics, X-rays, are all used to look for cracks in the structure, and nothing escapes inspection. Stripping a Jumbo or a DC-10 in this way means putting the plane in a specially constructed dock which enables all parts of the

plane to be got at. The overhaul goes on night and day, seven days a week, for almost a month.

Engines need to be overhauled at more frequent intervals, and can be removed for this purpose. They can then be shipped to a workshop specializing in turbine maintenance or even air freighted abroad. Boeing 707 operators once developed a system for slinging spare engines underneath the wings, and they could even be carried across the Atlantic in this way.

Our plane is now almost ready to leave once more, but there is time in hand; the new flight hasn't been called yet. So, while we are waiting we can have a look around at some of the other aeroplanes.

Soviet-built airliners are now fairly regular visitors to British airports, particularly the long-range four-engined Ilyushin Il-62 (Aeroflot and LOT Polish), the handsome three-engined Tupolev Tu-154 (operated by the Romanian airline TAROM and by Balkan Bulgarian), and the smaller and earlier Tupolev Tu-134, with two rear-mounted engines. This type appears in the livery of almost all East European airlines, including the Yugoslav IT company, Aviogenex. In some respects, these Soviet planes have interesting peculiarities, but it is well to dispel some of the myths first.

The biggest myth is that these airliners, particularly the Il-62 and Tu-134 (which when they first appeared had glazed noses) are really converted bombers. Only the Tu-104 of the 1950s was originally a bomber, which probably gave rise to the myth in the first place. However, more modern airliners have since been designed, to double if necessary, perhaps not as bombers but as military transports capable of operating in forward areas. Hence the glazed nose, which could be used in wartime by a navigator/observer. Hence also the remarkable undercarriage fitted to many Soviet planes; four-wheel, or even six-wheel bogies carrying large, low-pressure tyres, capable of landing and taking off on gravel, packed earth, war-damaged or makeshift runways, with long, stalky, well-sprung legs which can kick backwards to ride over the worst of the bumps. Sinister, you might say. But not quite. Gravel and packed-earth runways are common throughout Eastern Europe and the USSR, particularly at the smaller airfields. The surfaces are baked hard in the dry summer and frozen solid in the icy grip of winter – so, who needs concrete?

All these wheels have to fold away somewhere, and the system adopted by Tupolev is to have the entire leg (four-wheel on the Tu-134, six-wheel on the Tu-154) swing backwards into a specially designed, streamlined wheel-bay built onto the trailing-edge of each wing. These characteristic wheel-bay fairings give the Tupolevs a spiky appearance which is complemented by yet another spike protruding forward from the top of the fin. This third spike houses VHF radio aerials.

Your ears are due for a shock if you happen to stand near a Soviet plane starting up. Instead of the electric starters used on Western aircraft, the Russians favour pneumatic starters. Each engine in turn is spun up by means of a very noisy blast of compressed air.

And another thing. Apart from the supersonic Tu-144 'Concordski', now withdrawn from service, the three-engined Tu-154 was the first modern Soviet airliner to be designed from the outset without glass windows in the nose. It was also the first apart from the Concordski to have

The Soviet-built YAK-40 is an interesting, small, short-haul airliner *(Czechoslovak Airlines)*

Commuter airliner. The Embraer 110P2 Bandeirante from Brazil
(Air Ecosse)

powered controls. Even the big four-engined Ilyushin Il-62 relies on human muscle to heave it around the sky!

It is often said that Aeroflot, the Soviet airline, is the world's largest, but what of the others? Do you rate the size of an airline on the size of its fleet, the number of passengers it carries, or the number of route-miles it flies? Measured in terms of unduplicated route miles, British Airways is the world's biggest international airline.

It is possible to classify airlines roughly according to size. Thus British Airways is definitely in the first division, operating big planes on big routes and using the big airports. Examples of second-division airlines are British Midland, Air UK, and Dan-Air which specialize in serving the smaller routes, often using turboprop aircraft such as Viscounts, 748s, Friendships and Heralds. Remember that most jets are uneconomical over short hops, the exceptions being the F-28 Fellowship and the new British Aerospace 146.

The third-division airlines are, one imagines, smaller still, but some of them nowadays are doing very good business and the term 'commuter airlines', imported from across the Atlantic, might describe them better. Loganair and Air Ecosse are two commuter airlines which have grown up with the Scottish oil boom. They fly oilmen up and down the country, sometimes on charter, sometimes on a scheduled basis, operating into and out of, not just Aberdeen, but just about anywhere that has a runway – Sanday or Scilly, Fair Isle or Fetlar.

The commuter airlines go about their business in a

Commuter aircraft, all of them powered by the Pratt and
Whitney PT6A turboprop:
Above left Embraer Bandeirante *(Air UK)*
Below left De Havilland Canada DHC-6 Twin Otter over the
Sullom Voe oil terminal in the Shetlands *(Loganair)*

Above right Shorts SD 3-30, from Belfast *(Loganair)*
Below right De Havilland Canada DHC-7 'Dash 7' *(Tyrolean
Airlines)*

Air taxis and business aircraft:
Above left Piper Aztec *(Keenair)*
Below left Beech Super King Air

Above right Piper Navajo Chieftain *(British Caledonian Airways)*
Below right Britten Norman Trislander *(British Caledonian Airways)*

different way from their bigger brothers. Traffic is light, but steady and profitable. The passengers are mostly 'regulars' and as in the local pub, the idea is to ensure that they keep coming back for more. No room for old biplanes here; the planes have to be brand spanking new – like the neat Brazilian-built 18-seater Embraer Bandeirante, or the De Havilland Canada Twin Otter, both of which are powered by Pratt and Whitney PT6A turboprops, and the Twin Otter in particular is at home on the short runways, sometimes gravel, found on these remote Scottish islands. The regular custom soon pays off the capital invested in buying new planes, and encourages a kind of mateyness you don't find aboard bigger planes. Even the name 'Air Ecosse' has a slightly tongue-in-cheek ring about it, reminiscent of the Auld Alliance between Scotland and France, which was a thorn in the flesh of the English in earlier times!

Even small planes have come a long way since the days of Rapides and Tiger Moths, and some of them are among the most interesting types you are likely to see around. For example, we mentioned the PT6A turboprop just a moment ago. This is a very modern small engine, which is produced in a variety of sizes and goes into a remarkable range of aeroplanes, from the 6 to 12-seater Beech King Air business plane, the Beech 99, Piper Cheyenne, Embraer Xingu, Embraer Bandeirante and its less sleek rivals, the Shorts SD 3-30 and the De Havilland Canada DHC-6 Twin Otter. Then there is the Twin Otter's four-engined big brother, the DHC-7 Dash 7. The three latter types are specially designed to use the smaller, more inaccessible airfields, a vital asset for commuter flying.

Going further down the scale you will find the air-taxis, 6 to 12-seater 'go anywhere' planes usually powered by a pair of 300-400 hp piston engines. The best known is the 6-seat, 200 mph Piper Aztec and the slightly bigger Piper Navajo and Navajo Chieftain; while the British-designed Islander and Trislander and that flying horsebox, the Shorts Skyvan, fill the need for small planes able to lift awkward loads into and out of awkward places.

It is becoming a big status symbol these days to train for a Private Pilot's Licence (PPL). At the many flying schools up and down the country training consists of about 40 hours at the controls of a small single-engined plane such as a Cessna 150 or a Piper Cherokee, but these planes can be fitted with most of the latest radio aids, and the basic PPL is only the start. From the basic licence, private pilots can go on to train for endorsements in night flying, various categories of instrument flying, and so on.

The company- or privately owned executive aircraft are often in a class of their own as regards interior elegance and sophistication. Some are prestigious toys or tax-write-offs for people or businesses with money to spare; others are hard-working planes which more than justify their keep. In Britain, the business-jet you are most likely to see will be the HS-125. Many are company-owned, and a firm at Luton, McAlpine Aviation, maintains a charter fleet of HS-125s for hire by anyone who wants to rent a jet for the day.

Air freight is big business these days too, and although some freight can be carried in the baggage holds on scheduled passenger flights, much of it is transported in specially built or adapted aircraft. The freight version of the 747 has a nose which hinges upwards; the Canadair CL-44 has a swing-tail and the Aerospacelines Super Guppy opens its front door to reveal a cavern big enough to transport Airbus wings, tails or fuselages across Europe to Toulouse. Converted military transports such as the Shorts Belfast or the Lockheed L-100, a civilian Hercules, make good freighters. Most freight is compact enough to be loaded through an enlarged side-door into quite an ordinary aircraft, and it is often convenient to pack freight onto net-covered pallets or into shaped, sealed containers.

The freighting companies you see dotted around the airport are in business not to transport the freight but to collect it into plane loads, which is the best way of saving costs. Freight-handling companies load it on board and the airline takes it away.

'Cleared Take-off'

The crew are on hand about an hour before the flight. The captain is recognizable by the wings on his jacket and by the four broad gold bars on his sleeves or epaulettes. He will occupy the left-hand seat on the flight deck and during the flight he is fully in command. The other flight-crew members have one, two or three stripes. These days most short-haul jets have a crew of only two; there is no need for a navigator or a flight engineer. The co-pilot in the right-hand seat has full dual controls, shares the flying and does most of the talking on the radio. There will also be a spare seat on the flight deck for use as required by an observer or by a training captain. Although most crew training these days is on simulators, all crew still have to undergo regular six-monthly checks, including medical and practical flying tests. If you talk to a pilot he will probably tell you that flying an aeroplane is easy; it's the paperwork which is difficult.

Although the crew will know before the flight how much weight they are meant to be carrying, the weather is likely to be the most important element in the calculations. Hot weather, strong winds, heavy rain, ice, snow, low cloud and fog all present different problems. Hot weather or a slippery runway will limit the take-off weight; crosswinds may make landing difficult. Fog will necessitate a diversion to wherever there is clearer weather, and strong headwinds will slow the flight and burn more fuel. At the heights at which jets fly, the headwinds can be blowing at over 100 miles an hour.

The captain files a *flight plan*, which is really an Air Traffic Control document stating his proposed route. On short flights there is no choice of route anyway; you just use the nearest convenient airways to get from one place to another and the route is the same each time. But on long flights it is possible to vary the route to take advantage of better weather conditions. For example, if there is a deep depression to the west of Ireland, the winds will be rotating round it anti-clockwise, so therefore, westbound trans-atlantic flights will get help from tailwinds if they go round the depression to the north, while eastbound flights are better going around the south side.

Taking the weather into account, the captain is able to calculate how much fuel he needs on the basis of so much for the flight, plus enough to allow for a diversion with an extra 45 minutes reserves. Hauling unnecessary fuel around the sky is expensive. Other calculations will now be made to determine the various take-off speeds, depending on the load and the condition of the runway.

The flight deck is a jungle of controls, levers, switches and instruments. When they take their seats, the crew begin to carry out a whole litany of checks to ensure that everything is working properly. They work from printed lists calling the checks out to one another...

'Overspeed limiters... ON.'

'Stick pusher dump valve... OFF.'

The captain will have exchanged courtesies with his cabin staff and with the flight dispatcher, who will be sorting out the remaining bits of paperwork. The passengers will be starting to board, making themselves comfortable in their seats. Baggage and cargo will be loaded and hatches secured. There will be an air of expectancy, with everybody hoping for a prompt getaway.

Delays in getting airborne are not always the fault of the airline. Getting a plane from A to B involves co-operation from, and smooth teamwork by, all kinds of people from firemen and baggage loaders to air traffic controllers and Customs officers. Industrial action by one group of employees or the other takes place from time to time, but probably the most infuriating cause of flight delays is industrial action by air traffic controllers. This usually results in an artificial restriction in the number of flights that can be handled over the country in question. When a

British Aerospace has full order books for its superb HS-125 business jet which is built at Chester. The latest version, the HS-125 700 is in every respect a mini airliner. It has turbofan engines and can carry up to 10 passengers over distances up to 2500 miles at 500 mph *(McAlpine Aviation)*

Loading palletized cargo through the nose of a 747 freighter
(A Japan Airlines Photograph)

pilot has filed a flight plan he is allocated a 'slot time' which he dare not miss, but for which he might have to wait hours.

It makes little difference whether the passengers wait in the terminal or on board the plane. In Spain in summer, both places are likely to be hot and uncomfortable, because on board the plane the air conditioning is meant to breathe the cold air six miles high, and is not designed to cope with conditions at ground level for long periods. Besides, running the air conditioning also means using the Auxiliary Power Unit which uses fuel, and if the tanks need topping-

up afterwards, the plane could miss its slot time and have to wait for another. Sometimes it is good psychology as far as the passengers are concerned to start the engines and taxi at least part of the way towards the runway.

In Britain, delays in getting away are more likely to be due to congestion at busy airports such as Heathrow. Unlike the United States of America, where planes queue up one after the other on a taxiway waiting to take off, the

Right above The night mail. Post Office workers load up an Air Ecosse Twin Otter. Note the registration G-MAIL
Right below A Boeing 707 freighter is loaded with general cargo *(Lufthansa)*

Specialized cargo aircraft:
Above The Lockheed L-100-30, an adaptation of the Hercules military plane

Below An Aerospacelines Super Guppy delivering Airbus wings (*Airbus Industrie*)

practice in Britain is for the control tower to tell the pilot when it should be OK for him to start his engines and begin to move away from the ramp.

Jets usually park nose-in to the ramp, and as they cannot reverse, they need to be pushed back by a large tractor called an airtug. The 'redcap' will have checked that everything is in order, including the 'ship's papers', the steps will be moved away and the stewardess will be trying to close the door. The airtug has connected its towbar to the aircraft's nosewheel, and an engineer standing nearby will be in contact with the captain through a plug-in headset. The engines can be started, more checks completed, then the captain gives the OK for pushback. When the plane has been pushed back far enough, the towbar is disconnected and the engines begin to roar in real earnest. At this point you will see the control surfaces waggle as the pilot checks each of them to ensure that they move easily. More noise from the engines now and the plane begins to inch forward under its own power and move out along the taxiways.

'Speedbird Four Five Seven Two is cleared to the holding point, Runway Two Eight Left.'

The runway numbers refer to the compass direction in which they run. Heathrow's two parallel runways are aligned in the direction 278° looking westward and 098° if you look east. Round these directions to the nearest ten degrees and lop off the final nought and you get 28 painted at one end of the runways and 10 painted on the concrete at the other. The 'left' and 'right' bit is obvious.

'Speedbird Four Five Seven Two, your clearance is to Belfast via the Airways Amber One and Red Three on a Daventry One Foxtrot Standard Instrument Departure. Squawk Double Two Four Zero.'

The Airways Amber One and Red Three are standard routes via radio beacons which will take the plane to Belfast. The Daventry One Foxtrot routine is a kind of aerial slip-road, a safe route from the end of the runway to join the airways system at the Daventry radio beacon.

The 'squawk' is a radar identification code which the crew will dial on the aircraft's transponder: a four-figure number, in this case 2240. The transponder keeps on transmitting this code which will appear on air-traffic control radar screens alongside the blip which represents the aircraft.

At the Holding Point, a short distance back from the runway, the plane waits until the runway is clear.

'Speedbird Four Five Seven Two, line up and hold.'

The plane moves forward and turns onto the runway, then parks with the brakes on.

'Speedbird Four Five Seven Two is cleared take-off.'

The captain acknowledges and as he does so his right hand is pushing the power levers forward and the engines roar up to full power. Off come the brakes and the plane starts accelerating down the runway, with the captain's left hand on the nosewheel tiller keeping the plane straight, the co-pilot pushes the wheel forward to keep the nose down. The airspeed begins to register on the indicator.

'Vee One.'

This is the point of no return. The plane is now committed to take off. Should an engine fail now there would be no chance of stopping the plane before it ran out of runway, but it would be possible to get airborne and go round safely.

'Rotate.'

The captain allows the wheel to come back slightly and the nose rises. The main wheels leave the runway and the plane is airborne and climbing steeply, the wheels tuck themselves away and the undercarriage doors close.

The steep climb seems to flatten out almost as soon as the plane has crossed the airport boundary. The pilot has reduced the power in order to lessen the noise out of consideration for the inhabitants of Slough down below. By now the plane has begun its turn to the north, and the pilot has re-tuned his radio from the frequency of Heathrow tower to that of the area controller, hunched over his radarscope at West Drayton.

'Speedbird Four Five Seven Two. Good morning. Squawk ident.'

The pilot pushes the 'ident' button on the transponder and the blip on the controller's radar starts flashing. The numbers 2240 beside it disappear and are replaced with the aircraft's flight number BA4572. Also on the screen beside the blip are the numbers 59, indicating that the plane has reached an altitude of 5900 feet, and the letters AA, which signify that the flight's destination is Belfast. Isn't technology wonderful!

'Speedbird Four Five Seven Two cleared to flight level

one four zero. Your own navigation now, direct to Daventry.'

The captain punches a few buttons on the autopilot and the plane turns itself gently and smoothly onto a course for Daventry, climbing under full cruising power, first up to 14,000 feet, and then, under further instructions from the controller, all the way up to 29,000 feet, which it will maintain most of the way to Belfast. The network of airways is marked out by a pattern of radio beacons, some of which are inconspicuous little transmitters hidden away in a corner of some farmer's field; others are rather more spectacular. Provided that the crew give it the right instructions, the Trident's autopilot will use these beacons to get itself to Belfast.

To the crew, it's just another shuttle flight. Most of their work for the time being will consist of listening out for the controller's instructions over the radio, using the other radio to call up British Airways in Belfast to give them details of the flight, to confirm that the aircraft is fully serviceable and to order fuel for the return. That, and

Left The sharp end. A view across the flight deck of a Boeing 747. Despite the plane's size and complexity, the controls and instruments are neatly and logically laid out *(A British Airways Photograph)*

A 747 departs from a wet runway *(Air India Picture Library)*

keeping an eye on the autopilot to make sure it behaves itself, is all that the crew will be doing until they get close to the Isle of Man.

The cabin crew are busy serving refreshments and drinks to the passengers who are awake. Most of the passengers will be experienced air travellers, but there will be one or two, mostly younger, for whom the experience of flying will be a novel one. Five and a half miles up in the sky, the height of Mount Everest, where the air is so thin that most people would lose consciousness in seconds, and racing along at a speed of 550 mph – one mile every six and a half seconds – it's not natural. If God had meant humans to

The flight crew climbs aboard a Trident at the start of another shuttle flight from Manchester to Heathrow. This popular aeroplane has been the mainstay of British Airways' short- and medium-haul operations since 1964 and has pioneered the use of automatic landing systems in fog

Right above The Trident's American look-alike, the Boeing 727, has outsold any other airliner in modern times. A total of over 1500 727s of all versions have been produced *(Dan Air Services Limited)*
Right below An airtug at work

'Cleared take-off....' The magic moment when the captain pushes the power levers forward and releases the brakes. Gatwick's Runway 26 begins to be swallowed up *(British Caledonian Airways)*

The long view of this DC-10 is reflected from the heat-haze as it 'rotates' into the take-off attitude *(British Caledonian Airways)*

fly he would have given them wings instead of expecting them to roar around cooped up in these pressurized metal monsters, guzzling the Earth's resources at the rate of litres per second.

Outside the plane, the onrushing air as it passes over the wings is accelerated to a speed close to that of sound, but the sweepback deflects the pressure wave and allows it to escape. Twin vortices form in the slipstream as the plane passes, and the heat from the Rolls Royce Speys upsets the stability of the supercooled air and the vapour condenses out. Far below, the plane's tumult can scarcely be heard until it is already past, and the mark of its passing is a thin white line chalked in the blue sky over Cheshire.

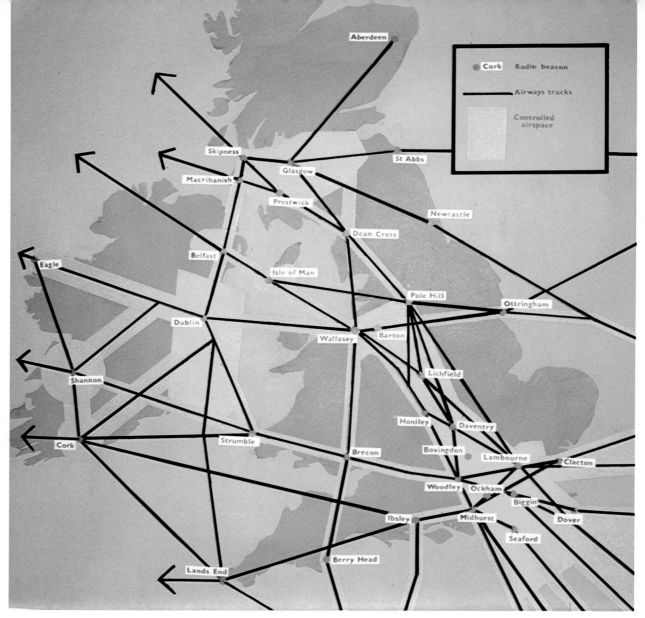

Simplified sketch-map showing the principal radio beacons, airways and zones and corridors of controlled airspace

Right above Air traffic controllers at their radarscopes
(Plessey Radar Limited)
Right below the Pole Hill radio beacon

Index